DIESEL HYDRAULICS

in the 1960s and 1970s

JOHN JENNISON and TONY SHEFFIELD

Ian Allan PUBLISHING

First published 2014

ISBN 978 0 7110 3745 8

Published by Ian Allan Publishing Ltd, Hersham, Surrey KT12 4RG

Printed in China

Visit the Ian Allan Publishing website at www.ianallanpublishing.com

FRONT COVER The flat windscreens on the 'Westerns' did not clear water particularly well and a number of experiments were undertaken to improve the situation, one of which was a clear rotating disc fitted in front of the driver, similar to that used on ships. This was called the 'Clear View Screen' and used an electric motor to rotate it. The first was fitted to No D1039 from March to December 1964, and a larger version was tried on No D1006 *Western Stalwart* from November 1965 until early 1967. Although generally satisfactory in dealing with heavy rain, the restricted vision was felt to counteract any advantage gained.

No D1006 was photographed ready to depart from Cheltenham St James on 27 November 1965 on what was described as the last steam-hauled service from Paddington, with No 7029 *Clun Castle* taking the train to Bristol, then up to Gloucester; there it handed over to the 'Western', which worked only the short distance to Cheltenham and return, handing back to No 7029 for the next leg to Swindon before two English Electric Type 3s returned the special to London. *www.rail-online.co.uk*

BACK COVER No D1058 *Western Nobleman* is attracting haulage fans in its final months in a classic view taken at Teignmouth on 13 November 1976 as it worked 1Z15, the 07.40 Paddington to Plymouth 'Footex'. It returned the train to the capital at 18.45, but only as far as Reading, where No 47505 was attached because *Western Nobleman* had suffered damage to its 'A'-end engine. No D1058 was withdrawn from service on 20 January 1977. *www.rail-online.co.uk*

TITLE PAGE 'Hymek' No D7002 and Type 2 No D6318 both display their stock numbers in the train indicator panels. This picture may have been taken in 1972 after both locomotives had been withdrawn and moved from St Phillip's Marsh to Swindon Works for scrapping on 3 February. No D7002 was never repainted and retained its small yellow warning panel to the end, whereas No D6318 acquired the second version of Rail Blue with full yellow ends and serif numbers.

BELOW Blue-liveried 'Hymek' No D7027, pictured at Reading in August 1968, had been transferred to Old Oak Common four months earlier. It was one of the most-travelled members of the class, being reallocated no fewer than ten times before withdrawal at Old Oak in November 1971. It had previously been there in 1964 and returned via Bristol Bath Road, Plymouth Laira and Landore. *www.rail-online.co.uk*

Contents

Introduction

The Western Region (WR) diesel-hydraulics were in service with British Railways for less than 20 years and were controversial throughout that time, both internally within British Railways and even more vocally in both the professional and enthusiast press. In this book we follow the fleet year by year from the optimism of the late 1950s and early 1960s through middle age to their final demise in 1977.

In 1959, R. A. Smeddle, the WR Chief Mechanical & Electrical Engineer, explained the rationale behind the Region's decision to pursue a different path from the rest of the network: 'Whilst in the early days of modernisation the tendency generally on British Railways was to develop designs for Diesel-Electric Locomotives, the Western Region Management was considering the possible advantage of the hydraulic transmission, and it was decided, with the concurrence of the British Transport Commission, that this Region should, in fact, take the initiative in exploring the possibilities in this field'. The WR senior management believed it was much more logical to build a 2,000hp locomotive weighing less than 80 tons using hydraulic transmission rather than a diesel-electric of more than 130 tons. Also, hydraulic transmission would be more suited to the haulage of heavy loads on steeply graded lines such as its South Devon main line.

Perhaps also behind these words was the tendency of the WR management for independence and keeping the spirit of the old Great Western Railway alive, albeit putting forward a rational scientific case based on the work done in Germany to develop hydraulic transmissions that, by the early 1950s, were well-established and successful.

Not only were the transmission systems different on the WR, but liveries were also the subject of variation. From their introduction through to the late 1960s the WR locomotives exhibited a variety of both colour and style. 'Warships' and 'Westerns' could be seen in green and maroon as well as Corporate Blue, with and without yellow warning panels and full yellow ends.

Furthermore, the quality of external appearance deteriorated rapidly as classes were run down or locomotives awaited a repaint, and this was more evident on the WR than any other region, with enthusiasts often commenting that it was due to the close proximity of the sea at Dawlish. However, the truth was that with train locomotives used to stable their own coaching stock, coupled with the aggressive carriage cleaning chemicals used in the automatic washing plants and perhaps poor final top-coat finishes, the locomotives were subjected to a form of chemical stripping. Parent depot Laira was well aware of this and started repainting 'Westerns' and even two 'Warships' as their condition became embarrassing.

The D600 and D800 'Warships'

When in May 1955 the BTC announced the approval of a Pilot Scheme for main-line diesels, 11 diesel-hydraulics were included, five of 2000hp and six of 1,000hp, all to be built by the North British Locomotive Company (NBL) using German Voith transmissions and MAN engines manufactured under licence. Unfortunately the BTC central staff engineers vetoed the lightweight four-axle German Railways V200 design that the WR wanted and insisted on a six-axle 117-ton locomotive of conventional design, the D600s.

However, the WR was still determined to get the machine it really wanted and managed to have three more 2,000hp locomotives added to the Pilot Scheme. These were closely based on the V200, essentially in a cut-down form to fit the British loading gauge. Before these entered service the BR Modernisation Plan was accelerated and large-scale orders were placed for locomotive types that were still on the drawing board, including another 30 diesel-hydraulics from Swindon similar to the three under construction. These became the D800s, and a further batch to the same design was also ordered from NBL.

The NBL Type 2 D6300s

The Western Region required a Type 2 diesel for local passenger and freight duties, and six were ordered from the North British Locomotive Company under the Pilot Scheme. Mechanically they were very similar to the D600s, using conventional heavy underframes, and they used the same MAN engines. As with the 'Warships', further locomotives were ordered before the prototype batch entered service. Initially, the majority of the class were based in the South West to cover their intended function on secondary work in Devon and Cornwall, with more than 20 transferring to Old

Oak Common in late 1963 and early 1964 for use on empty coaching stock trains and local freight work.

Designated as Class 22 under the TOPS scheme, the Type 2s were undoubtedly more successful than their D6100 diesel-electric counterparts, but the policy to eliminate all of the diesel-hydraulics would see their extinction by early 1972. Displaced from Old Oak by Class 31s, they saw out their final days in the West Country. One of the class was earmarked for private preservation but due to an administrative error was scrapped, the potential purchasers being offered a 'Warship' in its place!

The 'Hymeks'

The Type 3 'Hymeks' were the hydraulic replacement for the mixed-traffic 'Hall' and 'Grange' 4-6-0s. They were built by a consortium led by Beyer-Peacock at the latter's Gorton Works in Manchester. As with the 'Westerns', their external appearance benefited from the work of external design consultants, and with their two-tone green livery the result was one of the best-looking of all the first-generation main-line diesels.

The Western Region enthusiastically deployed the early locomotives as replacements for 'Castles' pending delivery of the more appropriate D1000s. However, the class soon began to develop serious transmission problems and it was almost a year before effective remedies were found. They reverted to more mundane work on less prestigious secondary passenger work as well as parcels and freight operation throughout the region, with high concentrations at Bristol Bath Road and Old Oak Common.

The large number originally based at Landore and Cardiff Canton were displaced on South Wales freight duties by English Electric Type 3s, although they did return there in quantity in 1967 when many of the diesel-electrics were transferred to the Eastern Region. The 'Hymeks' became Class 35 under TOPS but were not renumbered and were taken out of service from 1971 onwards, the last examples being withdrawn in 1975.

The 'Westerns'

Even before the 'Warships' had been delivered, in 1957 the WR management was looking for a locomotive that was more powerful and capable of handling its express services at higher speeds without reducing the loadings. Again they looked to Germany where a 3,000hp six-axle hydraulic had been introduced, and although the Germans again provided considerable technical help, the detailed design was done at Swindon, producing a completely original locomotive. Construction was to be shared between Swindon and Crewe Works, because the former was still completing production of the 'Warships'.

The resultant locomotives were arguably the most stylish of all BR's diesels and were a vindication of the BR Design Panel and the industrial design consultants who worked with it. The appearance of the 'Westerns' with their flat-fronted cab and large windows was a considerable departure from that of the 'Warships', and the interest of the railway enthusiasts of the day was increased by the decision to experiment with alternative liveries on the first few locomotives. The professional press was equally impressed, with the March 1962 issue of *Modern Railways* saying that the design featured 'the highest standard of diesel locomotive bodyform ever produced in this country' and was 'possibly without peer anywhere in the world today'. The entire class was to remain in service until 1973, by which time they were the sole remaining WR hydraulics, generating a cult following among enthusiasts from that point until final withdrawal came early in 1977.

The D9500s

If ever a class was introduced too late it was the D9500 650bhp Type 1 0-6-0. Design work on these began in early 1960 and by the time the first locomotives emerged from Swindon in July 1964 the traffic for which they were intended was in terminal decline. They became Class 14 under TOPS but none survived in service long enough to be renumbered.

Their centre-cab design provided a good view in both running directions, which was an advantage in a locomotive intended for shunting and transfer freight work. Unlike any of the other hydraulics they employed heavy steel plate frames and deep bufferbeams that resembled those of a GWR pannier tank more than the lightweight construction of the other classes.

Most of the D9500s were based in the South West at Bristol Bath Road or in South Wales, apart from a brief and unsuccessful flirtation

with four of the class at Old Oak Common as replacements for the '15xx' panniers. Their Paxman engines quickly proved unreliable and by early 1966 increasing numbers were placed in store. The Western Region somehow persuaded the Eastern Region to spare its embarrassment by taking 20 of them in January 1967 for use on dock trip workings at Hull.

On their home territory the first withdrawals came at the end of that year and the Eastern followed that example and withdrew its whole allocation on 1 April 1968. The last few at work in South Wales succumbed a year later. However, most of the class escaped the cutter's torch and were sold for industrial use, mainly to the National Coal Board or the British Steel Corporation, where they worked until the late 1980s and must have been a bargain for their purchasers, at least with regard to the original purchase price, as they were practically just 'run-in' when sold.

ABOVE Arguably the two best-looking diesel designs produced by British Railways, both the 'Westerns' and 'Hymeks' benefited from the input from external design consultants to transform what could otherwise have been a dull box-like shape into distinctive and stylish locomotives. Pictured on shed at Swindon on 8 June 1969, No D1014 *Western Leviathan* would remain in maroon until May 1970, while No D7005 kept this green livery until withdrawn in July 1972. *www.rail-online.co.uk*

Acknowledgements

This book is primarily about photographs and to produce it we have drawn primarily on the collection of Rail-Online (www.rail-online.co. uk). Our thanks go to Mark Alden, Martin Street and Roger Geach for their input to the captions, and to Colin Moss who has also provided a number of photographs from his own collection.

1 The early years, 1959-62

1959

ABOVE No D801 *Vanguard*, seen at Old Oak Common in October 1959, was the second of the three Swindon-built 'Warships' ordered under the British Railways Pilot Scheme, and illustrates the rather drab front-end appearance of the early D800s. The three Pilot Scheme and the first ten production series 'Warships' originally had GWR-style frames built into the nose doors to carry the train reporting numbers and reversible white train classification discs. Nos D800-2 were built with short curved horizontal grab rails below the front windows; these were replaced by the longer type used on D803-70 when route indicator panels were fitted. The 'Warships' built at Swindon had oval brass works plates, with a light grey background and red letters and numbers, fixed on the centre line of the side skirt immediately above the tanks. Other details to note are the rubber kicking pads below the cab doors, which were replaced in 1960, and the red marker light below the upper lamp bracket. The Western Region gave the D800s Red route availability, the same as a GWR 'Castle', and as with the steam locomotives a 4½-inch red disc was applied to the cab sides at both ends, positioned directly below the numbers on the access panels. No D801 gained yellow warning panels in February 1962, and a four-character route indicator panel in October 1963. *MIS*

1960

ABOVE A pair of Type 2s are seen at Swindon shed in December 1960 after both had been in the Works for repairs. No D6321 had been delivered from North British in April and had completed a Light Classified repair, while No D6331, which was delivered only in July, had been stopped for an Unclassified repair.
www.rail-online.co.uk

FACING PAGE TOP The passengers bustle around prior to departure from Penzance on 21 August 1960. Although No D824 *Highflyer* had only entered traffic four weeks earlier, the absence of a yellow warning panel leaves the front end of the 'Warship' looking quite unattractive. The route indicator panel is not in use for this Sunday train. *GTS*

FACING PAGE BOTTOM No D845 *Sprightly*, at Truro in April 1961 with the 10.00am Penzance-Paddington 'Cornish Riviera', had just been delivered from the North British Locomotive Company in Glasgow. It was the first 'Warship' to receive a yellow warning panel when it was returned to traffic after a casual repair at Swindon at the end of August 1961. At the same time it was also given thin white crescents at the front of the cab roofs, but these were not applied to any other member of the class. It is many years since this platform was in use as a through platform; Truro was rationalised during 1971 with the West signal box taken out of use and the yard remodelled. A large 'Portakabin'-type building was placed across the lines at the London end where No D845 stands and this became the home of the British Rail Area Manager Truro and his staff. *CTLS*

1961

ABOVE The classic Great Western photograph – this is probably very close to how the GWR would have produced a diesel if nationalisation hadn't got in the way in 1948. In green livery and hauling a train of 'chocolate and cream' coaches, No D829 *Magpie* passes a sparsely populated beach at Dawlish on 24 July 1961 with the 9.00am Wolverhampton-Penzance train. *H. Ramsey*

LEFT The first North British-built 'Warship', No D600 *Active*, stands at Old Oak Common on 12 November 1961 alongside the first production 'Warship' from Swindon, No D803 *Albion*. The D600s would only be found in the capital for another six months or so, after which they were restricted to working west of Newton Abbot. *Active* has gained the train reporting number frame and vertical louvres since it was introduced in January 1958. It received full BR Corporate Blue in April 1967, only months before the whole class was withdrawn at the end of that year. *www.rail-online.co.uk*

ABOVE Standing outside Swindon 'A' Shop, No D6326 had been delivered from North British in May 1960 but was stopped at Laira a month later and sent to Swindon for Unclassified attention, which kept it out of service until early August. The four diamond-shaped aluminium North British Locomotive Company maker's plates, placed below the cab numbers, can be clearly seen. No D6326 was one of the last D6300s in service, surviving until October 1971, by then in Rail Blue with full yellow ends, and during that final summer was a regular sight working around the Exeter area on freight, vans and even the occasional passenger service. *www.rail-online.co.uk*

ABOVE The appearance of the 'Hymek' in both styling and livery owes much to the input of Ted Wilkes, of the consultants Wilkes & Ashmore, who advised the BR designers. No D7003 arrived at Swindon on 30 July 1961 from Beyer-Peacock's works at Gorton, Manchester, and entered traffic on 3 August, allocated to Bristol Bath Road. *www.rail-online.co.uk*

RIGHT Hymek No D7001 was only a few weeks old when this picture was taken at Bath Spa – it had entered service on 3 July 1961. The first three of the class did not have the air horns on the cab roof when built; instead they were located under the buffer beam.
www.rail-online.co.uk

LEFT One of the final batch of Swindon-built 'Warships', No D867 *Zenith*, is seen at Swindon. The picture was probably taken after completion of a Light Classified repair on 1 August 1962, during which it gained its yellow warning panels. Its bufferbeam is painted in that rather peculiar orange-red colour; although the green on the nose has been repainted, the bodyside paintwork has not been retouched. The red-backed 83D shed plate was used for Plymouth Laira until September 1963, when the depot became 84A. *T. Berry*

ABOVE The last 'Warship', No D870 *Zulu*, was to be the subject of a trial fitting of electric train heating, which would involve increasing the level of turbo-charging by using intercoolers to produce the additional power needed. The experiment was aborted while No D870 was still under construction, leaving as the only visible sign the moving of the Desilux air horns to a fibreglass cowling at the front edge of the cab roof to make space for the ETH jumper cables below the buffer beam. *Zulu* is nearing completion on 24 September 1961 as the first two 'Westerns', Nos D1000 and D1001, take shape alongside. To the left of the picture is the replica GWR broad-gauge *North Star*. No D870 entered service on 25 October and No D1000 *Western Enterprise* on 20 December, but No D1001 *Western Pathfinder* remained at Swindon until February 1962. *www.rail-online.co.uk*

ABOVE No D1001 *Western Pathfinder* is seen at Old Oak Common in original condition, which lasted until October 1962, when it received a yellow warning panel. The first maroon locomotives from both Swindon (Nos D1001/5-10) and Crewe (Nos D1039-43) did not have yellow warning panels and had yellow bufferbeams and buffer stocks. All later locomotives were built with yellow warning panels on the cab front and the bufferbeam, and the stocks were painted black. No D1001 was the only one of the class to have white window pillars; they were light grey on all subsequent locomotives. *www.rail-online.co.uk*

1962

ABOVE Two North British-built 'Warships', Nos D862 *Viking* and D857 *Undaunted*, double-head the 8.30am Paddington-Penzance 'Royal Duchy' into Cornwall across Brunel's Royal Albert Bridge over the River Tamar at Saltash in late March or early April 1962. No D862 was newly delivered from NBL at Glasgow earlier in the month, while No D857 had been in traffic since November 1961. *www.rail-online.co.uk*

RIGHT The two 'Warships' are seen moments later as they pass through Saltash station. No D862 still has its newly built shine, while No D857 has weathered slightly during its four months in traffic. The 'chocolate and cream' Mark 1 coach blends nicely with the green livery of the 'Warships'. *www.rail-online.co.uk*

ABOVE No D1004 *Western Crusader* was only a month old when this picture was taken by the entrance to the old steam shed at Laira on 20 June 1962. Three Swindon-built and four Crewe-built 'Westerns' originally had this green livery, and No D1004 was one of only three never to carry maroon livery, going straight into blue in February 1967. *www.rail-online.co.uk*

ABOVE No D6316 stands at Swindon Works on 12 August 1962 with Nos D6340 and D6341. The older locomotive, which had been in service since March 1960, has been sent up from Laira for a Heavy Classified repair, which lasted until 10 October. It has already been given a yellow warning panel at its home depot but has not yet been fitted with route indicator boxes. The reason for the presence of the other two D6300s is more interesting; No D6340 had entered traffic on 3 April 1962 and No D6341 on 12 May 1962, and despite the fact that they were only just about run-in both would receive Heavy Classified Repairs, completed on 29 November and 13 November 1962 respectively. The deliveries of the final Type 2s were severely delayed by a combination of NBL's precarious financial position and BR's request to concentrate production on the final 'Warships'. There was a gap of nine months between the delivery of No D6336 in July 1961 and No D6337 in March 1962. It is likely that the build quality of a number of these diesels, the last to emerge from NBL, was not up to standard and hence significant rectification work had to be carried out on them at Swindon. The same issues applied to one other member of the class, No D6346, which also underwent a similar repair at Swindon from July to November, after less than two months in service. Note on No D6316 the red-backed 83A shed plate, the brass North British diamond maker's plate and the yellow route code disc; the other two locomotives have aluminium plates and were built with route indicator boxes. *www.rail-online.co.uk*

ABOVE No D849 *Superb* heads the 11.40am Birkenhead-Paddington service at Leamington on 5 October 1962. It was delivered from North British in April 1961 and has that company's traditional black diamond maker's plate with polished letters and numbers, positioned on the centre line of the side skirt immediately above the tanks. 'Warships' were used on the Paddington-West Midlands line at this date because delays in delivery meant that there were only 17 'Westerns' in traffic when full dieselisation of the route commenced on 10 September

1962. The latter also had cyclic diagrams including South Wales and Plymouth services, so there were insufficient in traffic to cover requirements. The Western Region operating department had proposed to retain four 'Kings' for short-term cover, but the General Manager, Stanley Raymond, vetoed that and 'Warships' were used until sufficient numbers of the new locomotives were in service. When not on passenger duty, the locomotives were used by Wolverhampton Oxley depot on its freight diagrams. *CTLS*

2 The mid-1960s

1963

ABOVE No D1000 *Western Enterprise*, outside the Erecting Shop at Swindon Works, is in its original desert sand livery and has the yellow warning panels it carried between November 1962 and October 1964. Desert sand had been proposed for the Eastern Region's 'Deltics' by George Williams, the British Transport Commission Design Officer, but was rejected in favour of two-tone green. It was one of two colours, the other being turquoise blue, favoured by Williams and Misha Black, the design consultant responsible for the styling of the 'Westerns'. Two other schemes were proposed by Black at the same time,

standard locomotive green and a bright shade of red. Seven of the class duly entered service in green, but the Western Region General Manager, Stanley Raymond, decided in August 1962 that the 'Standard Coaching Maroon' first used on No D1001 would be standardised for the rest of the fleet, leaving No D1000 in splendid isolation. *Western Enterprise*, which had slightly larger nameplates than its classmates, was the only member of the class to carry cast aluminium crests, identical to those used on the London Midland Region electric locomotives, which it kept even after repainting in maroon, although they were removed when it went into Rail Blue in June 1967.
www.rail-online.co.uk

ABOVE Green-liveried No D1003 *Western Pioneer* heads the 7.40am Birkenhead Woodside-Paddington service at Wellington, Shropshire, on 7 April 1963. The train would be strengthened at Wolverhampton Low Level with another three coaches for the onward journey to Paddington. No D1003 stayed in this livery until a works visit for an Intermediate overhaul starting in August 1965, following which it emerged in maroon. *www.rail-online.co.uk*

ABOVE A veritable feast of green hydraulics at Bristol Bath Road on 28 July 1963 – four D6300s, three 'Hymeks' and a 'Warship' are visible, and not a diesel-electric in sight. Nearest the camera is No D6356, the penultimate Type 2, which had been allocated to Bath Road from new in July 1962 and stayed until October 1964 when it moved to Old Oak Common. Together with Cardiff Canton and Plymouth Laira, the Bristol depot was one of three equipped for 'Heavy' maintenance, which required facilities to lift diesel-hydraulic engines and transmissions, and train-heating boilers. However, Bath Road depot could not undertake bogie changes or tyre-turning, so locomotives needing attention to bogies or wheels were sent to Laira or Canton. *www.rail-online.co.uk*

ABOVE No D1047 *Western Lord* and No D870 *Zulu* were photographed at Swindon Works on 5 May 1963, and it was during this visit that the latter was given its yellow warning panel; it was released the following day back into traffic. No D1047 was in the works three times in six months during 1964 for Unclassified repairs to its cardan shaft and intermediate final drive. The final 'Warship' was easily recognised by the fibreglass cowling at the front edge of the cab roof. *www.rail-online.co.uk*

RIGHT Almost all of the North British Type 2s were originally allocated in the South West, to either Newton Abbot or Laira. On 24 August 1963 No D6310 arrives at Camborne with a local passenger train. Built in January 1960, it would receive small yellow warning panels at its next visit to Swindon, but it was never to carry blue livery, being withdrawn in green during March 1971.
www.rail-online.co.uk

LEFT A rare picture of two 'Westerns' on shed at Carmarthen on 29 September 1963. One would be employed on the daily Whitland to Kensington Olympia milk train, running light to and from Whitland.
www.rail-online.co.uk

1964

ABOVE No D1002 *Western Explorer* emerges from Box Tunnel with a Bristol-bound train on 12 July 1964. Built in green livery with red-backed nameplates, it was repainted in maroon during an Unclassified overhaul at Swindon from March to May 1965. *www.rail-online.co.uk*

TOP RIGHT No D1057 *Western Chieftain* stands at Bristol Bath Road on 12 July 1964 with another 'Western' and two 'Hymeks' behind. No D1057 was repainted in blue with small yellow warning panels in January 1967 and was the last of those carrying this livery to go into blue with full yellow ends, in January 1972. By the time it entered Swindon Works in September 1971 it had very badly worn paintwork and looked almost white down one side. *www.rail-online.co.uk*

BOTTOM RIGHT No D1069 *Western Vanguard* arrives at Cardiff on 13 July 1964 with a London-bound train – an all-maroon ensemble. The 'Western' was built at Crewe, entering traffic in October 1963, and was originally allocated to Canton before moving to Landore in March 1964. *www.rail-online.co.uk*

LEFT **LEFT** No D1019 *Western Challenger* speeds through Wellington (Somerset) with a westbound express on 14 July 1964. It was one of four of the class, Nos D1017-20, that were not modified with dual AWS and air brake equipment in the early 1970s, and this led to its withdrawal in May 1973. *www.rail-online.co.uk*

RIGHT D823 *Hermes* is also seen at Wellington on the same day, roaring through the station with the 11.50am Penzance-Paddington 'Royal Duchy'. Pannier tank No 9663 waits in the bay on the left as its driver has a chat with the man on the trackside. *www.rail-online.co.uk*

LEFT Still in the golden ochre livery, which lasted until late 1965, No D1015 *Western Champion* enters Exeter St David's on 15 July 1964. The livery was proposed by Brian Haresnape as an alternative to the standard British Railways diesel green, but was not taken up; *Western Champion* remained the sole example. In 1979 No D1015 was rescued, literally at the final hour before it was due to be cut up at Swindon, by the Diesel Traction Group. It was in appalling condition and after many years of effort and following what amounted to virtually a complete rebuild, the locomotive was restored to main-line condition in 2002 and has worked extensively on railtours since then. *www.rail-online.co.uk*

RIGHT No D1065 *Western Consort* heads the 8.30am Plymouth-Paddington 'Mayflower' at Dawlish in August 1964. It was delivered from Crewe in June 1963 but was badly damaged in a collision later that year and was unlucky enough to be involved in another collision in January 1972, resulting in a stay of almost eight months at Swindon Works.
www.rail-online.co.uk

ABOVE Paxman-engined Type 1 No D9513 is seen at Swindon Works on 27 September 1964 ready for its acceptance trials and then traffic – if there was any still available for it. *www.rail-online.co.uk*

TOP RIGHT One of the long-standing routes for the 'Hymeks' was that from Paddington to Worcester. No D7058 is pictured at Honeybourne on 16 April 1964 with an express to London. *www.rail-online.co.uk*

BOTTOM RIGHT Through working of 'Warships' into Crewe on expresses to Liverpool/Manchester from Bristol/Cardiff,

eliminating a locomotive change at Shrewsbury, began on 18 June with the 1962 Summer Timetable, and the North West-South West services were accelerated by up to 60 minutes. However, their working on these services was short-lived and by early 1964 they had been displaced by Brush Type 4s. No D825 *Intrepid* is on a Manchester-Plymouth train at Shrewsbury in 1963. *G. W. Sharpe*

1965

ABOVE No D9518 was new to Canton Cardiff on 30 October 1964 and is seen here doing the work for which it was designed, a freight trip working, probably from Radyr, in May 1965. Subsequently sold to the NCB for use at Ashington, it was out of use there by 1981 but remained on shed until 1987, when it was acquired for the Rutland Railway Museum near Cottesmore. Currently it resides at the West Somerset Railway. *CTLS*

FACING PAGE TOP One of the Old Oak Common fleet, No D6356, heads out of Paddington towards Royal Oak on 22 April 1965. It had arrived from Bristol Bath Road in October 1964 and worked on the Paddington ECS duties and local parcels and freight until May 1969, when it was transferred to Laira. By September 1969 No D6356 was in store, but was returned to traffic in December and ordered to Swindon for overhaul. It emerged in February 1970 repainted in blue livery, going back to Old Oak Common and finally Laira again from May 1971 until it was withdrawn in October. *www.rail-online.co.uk*

FACING PAGE BOTTOM The Type 2s were a familiar sight on Paddington empty coaching stock (ECS) duties from late 1963 until 1969. No D6354, pictured on 22 April 1965, had been transferred to Old Oak Common together with several other members of the class for this work. It arrived from Laira in September 1964 and stayed until January 1969, when it returned to the West Country at Newton Abbot as Brush Type 2s took over the D6300s' work. *www.rail-online.co.uk*

LEFT The first of the production series 'Warships' built at Swindon, D803 *Albion* idles away on the through road at Exeter Central. The picture was taken between February 1965, when it was fitted with four-character train identification indicators, and October 1967, when it entered the Works to emerge in blue livery. *www.rail-online.co.uk*

LEFT No D9544 is newly completed in Swindon Works on 31 May 1965, with the ironic 'OK44' headcode – all that was needed was some work for it! The Type 1 was officially allocated to Cardiff Canton on 29 May and worked in South Wales for just two years before being transferred to Hull Dairycoates in May 1967, where it enjoyed an even shorter period in traffic. No D9544 was withdrawn on 1 April 1968 and was subsequently sold to BSC Corby, based at its Gretton Brook shed. However, this locomotive was unlucky because it was cannibalised for spares and latterly dumped outside minus its wheels. Still wearing its British Railways livery and number, it was cut up on site in October 1980. *www.rail-online.co.uk*

ABOVE No D1019 *Western Challenger* departs from Paddington on 22 April with an express to Bristol. It would retain this livery until December 1969 when it received Corporate Blue. No D1019 was one of the four to remain vacuum-braked only and this would result in an early withdrawal for *Challenger*, on 6 May 1973, although it last worked only a few days earlier. *www.rail-online.co.uk*

ABOVE This view taken at Paddington, believed to be in 1965, contrasts the stylish appearance of the 'Westerns' with the more workmanlike front end of their 'Warship' predecessors. A Crewe-built 'Western' stands alongside No D859 *Vanquisher*, which was the only 'Warship' to have long side grab rails on the nose end. *www.rail-online.co.uk*

1966

ABOVE Type 1 No D9522, seen at Reading in 1966 on station pilot duties, is in excellent external condition despite being released for service in November 1964. The work for which this class had been designed had already declined, so there was a surplus of locomotives, probably resulting in few 'engine hours' during which No D9522 could get dirty. *www.rail-online.co.uk*

ABOVE No D6307 stands at Laira in the mid-1960s with the large high-mounted headcode boxes that were retro-fitted to Nos D6300-33. These were not successful and most of the locomotives, No D6307 being of the few exceptions, were modified with the flush-pattern indicator boxes that Nos D6334 onwards had from new. No D6307 was built in October 1959 and, apart from the addition of the yellow warning panel seen here, remained in green livery until taken out of traffic in May 1971. It was the second locomotive in the first production series of the class and, together with Nos D6306/8-12, had the 'eyebrow' air intakes above the cab windows in common with Nos D6300-06, although unlike the Pilot Scheme locomotives the windscreen wipers were mounted above rather than below the windows. No D6307 was one of a small number of the class to have cast brass rather than aluminium maker's plates. *www.rail-online.co.uk*

3 The late 1960s

1967

ABOVE A spotter fills his book with hydraulic numbers from this wonderful gathering around the Old Oak Common turntable on 12 February 1967. All four main-line types are represented, although the 'Western' on the left only just sneaks into the picture, and Brush Type 4 No D1756 is the only diesel-electric intruder. The identity of only two of the hydraulics was recorded by the photographer – 'Hymek' No D7081 and 'Warship' No D825 *Intrepid*. No D7081 caught fire at Bathampton in July 1971 while working a freight and was badly damaged; it was taken to Old Oak for storage before being officially withdrawn on 11 September. Although No D7006 was the first of the class to be taken out of service, on 2 September 1971, No D7081 was effectively the earliest casualty after only seven years and nine months in traffic. *www.rail-online.co.uk*

ABOVE No D9523 and friends are arranged around the turntable at Hull Dairycoates on 8 March 1967. It had arrived there on 20 January 1967, together with Nos D9512, D9551 and D9552, behind Class 37 No D6893, and was one of a total of 20 of the class transferred there at the end of 1966 from the Western Region, where the work for which they had been designed had almost completely dried up. Their poor reliability was no doubt another factor. The intention was to use them on the trip freights to the docks and the traffic from Hessle quarry to the Wilmington cement works. According to a member of staff based at Dairycoates, the management somewhat optimistically thought working costs would go down compared with the existing fleet; in fact, the reverse happened and costs went up because of engine problems, and many of the jobs had to be double-headed because the Type 1s did not have sufficient brake power for the loads they were asked to work. He also recalls the 'Paxmans' trundling along with the quarry trains, sometimes accompanied by loads of black clag and occasionally the odd flame coming from the exhausts. Monday mornings at Dairycoates were known as 'Thunderbirds Are Go', as it was often a bit of a rescue act to get the locomotives away into traffic as they had a habit of not wanting to start; this was often cured by a blast on the starter motor from the old brass fire extinguisher in the cab, which contained carbon tetrachloride.

Many of the locomotives that left Dairycoates for further use had attention from Dairycoates staff at their new homes. Most of this was minor modification or removal of some of the safety systems British Railways had fitted that the new owners did not require. *ExeRail*

ABOVE The paint is hardly dry on No D7064 at Swindon on 12 March 1967. The blue livery with white window surrounds suited the 'Hymeks' almost as much as the original two-tone green. No D7064 was one of a small number of the class to carry three different livery styles, ending its days in blue with full yellow ends. At the date of the picture it was allocated to Old Oak Common, in between two periods at its only other depot, Cardiff Canton. No D7064 was withdrawn in October 1971. *www.rail-online.co.uk*

ABOVE No D800 *Sir Brian Robertson* ticks over outside the running shed at Swindon on 12 March 1967. It was named after the Chairman of the British Transport Commission and was the only member of the class with a single-line name without the 'Warship Class' suffix below. As one of the first three non-standard 'Warships' it was an early withdrawal, in October 1968, remaining in green livery to the end, the only member of the class to do so. It received a four-character headcode panel and longer horizontal grab rails in March 1964. Interesting detail points to note are the red-backed cast 84A Laira shed plate on the left-hand fairing and the clip below the cab window to hold the driver's name. *www.rail-online.co.uk*

ABOVE Type 2 No D6343 heads a train of milk tanks at Kensington Olympia in April 1967, a typical duty for the London-based D6300s when they were not employed on Paddington ECS work. This locomotive was at Old Oak Common from May 1964 until May 1971, moving to Laira for its last six months in service. Its paintwork is looking rather tired and it was one of the class repainted into blue livery with full yellow ends. *www.rail-online.co.uk*

LEFT 'Warship' No D826 *Jupiter* is seen at Basingstoke on 10 May 1967 with a train of green-liveried stock, mostly of Southern Railway Bulleid origin, which had a more rounded profile than the British Railways Mark 1 coaches that closely followed their design. Although at first sight the headcode looks appropriate for the route, it is doubly incorrect – '1066' did not exist and possibly should have been '1086', because the locomotive working that Plymouth-Brighton train would often still carry that headcode when going forward from Salisbury on its next diagrammed train, the 14.35 Salisbury-Waterloo. No D826 was not repainted in maroon, going straight to blue in January 1968. *www.rail-online.co.uk*

RIGHT No D868 *Zephyr* leans into the curve at Basingstoke on 10 May 1967 with the 15.00 Waterloo to Exeter train. The Swindon-built 'Warships' took over the passenger workings on the Southern Region route to the West Country in August 1964 and had a virtual monopoly of these semi-fast services until October 1971; the North British locomotives made only very rare appearances as substitutes for failures, and then usually at the London end. No D868 kept its green livery until it went to Swindon in September 1967, emerging in blue with full yellow ends and serif numerals by the end of the year. *www.rail-online.co.uk*

RIGHT From the autumn of 1965 'Warships' repainted during Intermediate overhauls went into the same maroon livery as the 'Westerns', devoid of all lining and relieved only by the yellow warning panels. North British-built No D839 *Relentless*, which went into maroon in February 1966, was one of 32 'Warships' that eventually carried this livery. As can clearly be seen in this picture at Tiverton in 1967, the cab numbers were repositioned centrally below the cab windows, which allowed the red route availability discs to be moved up under the number and off the cab access flaps. These flaps were originally fixed at top and bottom with locks, which often seized and led to them not being properly secured; thus they often fell out as a result of vibration or movement.

The photograph clearly shows a number of front-end details. The class as built had a small oval-shaped grill located just outside the top right of the reporting numbers, which can be seen behind the lamp on the right; this was an air intake, and they were blanked off when electric demisters were introduced in 1965/66. Similar blanking plates were used on the bufferbeams to cover the holes left behind when the multiple working fittings were removed. *Relentless*, which shows signs of a slight altercation on the left-hand side, was allocated to Newton Abbot from June 1962 until September 1967, its 83A shed plate being visible on the skirting, although it had originally been positioned on the oval pad on the bufferbeam. It was one of 21 North British 'Warships' transferred to Old Oak Common in late 1967 to work freight and passenger services on the Paddington-Birmingham line, and freight services in and out of Bescot yard. *www.rail-online.co.uk*

ABOVE No D6354 and No D859 *Vanquisher* are seen during an Old Oak Common Open Day on 15 July 1967, both resplendent in the recently acquired early incarnation of Rail Blue with serif numbers and two sets of double arrows. For some reason that remains lost in the mists of time, *Vanquisher* was the only 'Warship' to have long side grab rails on the nose end. Class 22 No D6354 worked from Old Oak for another 18 months before the 81A hydraulic Type 2s were replaced by the diesel-electric Brush Type 2s transferred from the Eastern Region. *www.rail-online.co.uk*

LEFT 'Hymek' No D7015 is at Paignton on 15 July 1967 with Brush Type No D1934 in tow. The industrial shunter in the foreground is Ruston RH '48DS' class, works number 402809, in the headshunt of Hollacombe Gas Works. After this closed in 1968 the shunter was sent to Exeter Gasworks in August of that year. *www.rail-online.co.uk*

RIGHT No D1017 *Western Warrior* approaches Paignton on 15 July 1967 with the Saturdays-only 12.05 Paddington to Kingswear service, with the gas works in the background. Numerically this was the first of the four consecutively numbered 'Westerns' chosen to remain vacuum-braked, as there was no operational need to convert all 74 of the class to dual braking. This made them the first candidates for planned withdrawal when traffic needs declined further. No D1017 had received full yellow ends on 7 March 1968, and was withdrawn on 1 August 1973 after becoming the last survivor of the quartet. *www.rail-online.co.uk*

RIGHT No D1062 *Western Courier* heads the 10.50 Paddington to Paignton train, the 'Torbay Express', at Teignmouth on 19 July 1967. The 'Western' is clearly in need of its forthcoming repaint, but this would not happen until the following May when it went into Swindon to be fitted with dual air brakes and BR AWS, emerging in October in blue with full yellow ends. *Courier* was the first 'Western' to be preserved following withdrawal in August 1974. *www.rail-online.co.uk*

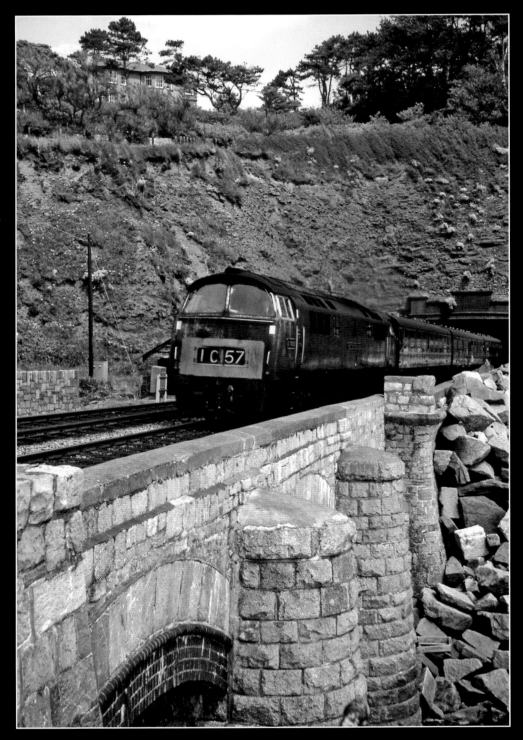

LEFT No D1013 *Western Ranger* works 4V29, the 03.11 Etruria (Stoke-on-Trent) to St Blazey clay empties, at Teignmouth on the same day as the picture opposite. This train was worked by 'Westerns' for many years and was a regular sight along the sea wall in the afternoon. Later in life *Western Ranger* would be instantly recognisable when its number and nameplates were painted with red backgrounds following attention at Laira during May 1976. *www.rail-online.co.uk*

RIGHT One of the more camera-shy 'Westerns', No D1024 *Western Huntsman*, emerges from the tunnel at Teignmouth, again on 19 July 1967, with 'The Cornishman', the 07.02 Bradford to Penzance train, which was due to pass there at around 14.20. Note the vents under the prow of the roof above the windows, to supply additional ventilation and only fitted to Nos D1004, D1024 and D1052. Unlike most Swindon-built 'Westerns', *Huntsman* has high-positioned Overhead Line warning flashes. *www.rail-online.co.uk*

LEFT At Old Oak Common in July 1967 are two locomotives newly repainted in Rail Blue. Class 35 No D7035 was ex-works from Swindon on 6 July 1967, and Class 22 No D6328 was released to traffic at about the same time. Both have 81A shed codes stencilled level with their numbers, inboard of the cab doors. The 'Hymek' has one centrally positioned double arrow whereas the Class 22 has one beneath each cab number. The repainted 'Hymeks', like the 'Westerns' with their cast number plates, kept their individual metal numbers. *www.rail-online.co.uk*

RIGHT Newly repainted in blue with full yellow ends and serif numbers, No D6332 is on show at the Bristol Bath Road depot Open Day on 15 July 1967. Note the 81A Old Oak Common shed plate on the front skirting and the NBL maker's plate now moved from the cabside to the centre of the solebar above the fuel tanks. No D6332 had been transferred to Old Oak from Newton Abbot in January 1966 and was withdrawn in May 1971. *www.rail-online.co.uk*

LEFT No D814 *Dragon* enters Newton Abbot on 24 June 1967 with the 07.40 Bristol West-Tavistock Junction freight. The 'Warship' was to be called to Swindon for an overhaul within a month, to emerge in blue towards the end of August. It had received the yellow warning panels in February 1963 and lost its multiple working fittings in early 1966.
www.rail-online.co.uk

RIGHT No D1069 *Western Vanguard* is seen in the early spring of 1967 near Taunton with the return Etruria (Stoke-on-Trent) to St Blazey china clay empties. Its paintwork is in a dreadful condition and it would go into the works for an Unclassified repair in April, emerging in blue with full yellow ends in 11 May.
www.rail-online.co.uk

RIGHT No D1062 *Western Courier*, seen at Bristol in 1967, already shows signs that it needs its next repaint at Swindon. However, the faded paintwork would have to last until the following year, when the locomotive went into blue with full yellow ends during a repair that lasted from May until October, when it was fitted with dual air brakes and the British Railways-pattern AWS. In the background an English Electric Class 40 is an interloper at the depot, a rare visitor from the London Midland Region.
www.rail-online.co.uk

RIGHT No D7040, pictured in 1967 at Bristol Temple Meads, was always allocated to Bath Road depot, and was withdrawn from there in this livery on 11 January 1972 as part of the National Traction plan, being switched off in working condition like sister loco No D7041. Both locomotives had entered traffic together and finished together, and were Bath Road engines for all of their working lives. *www.rail-online.co.uk*

LEFT No D800 *Sir Brian Robertson* waits to depart from Basingstoke in 1967. As one of the first three non-standard 'Warships', No D800 was an early withdrawal, in October 1968, remaining in green livery to the end, the only member of the class to do so. It had received a four-character headcode panel in March 1964. Two interesting detail points to note are the red-backed cast 84A Laira shed plate on the left-hand fairing and the clip below the open cab window to hold the driver's name. *www.rail-online.co.uk*

ABOVE In early 1964 the Western Region announced that the 'Westerns' were to be moved to the Paddington-Bristol and Paddington-Plymouth services, displacing 'Warships' and releasing them for other duties including dieselisation of the Southern Region Exeter-Salisbury-Waterloo route, which came under WR control from 7 September 1964. A regular-interval pattern of semi-fasts was introduced between Waterloo and Exeter to replace the express services hauled by the Bulleid 'Pacifics'. No D800 *Sir Brian Robertson*, pictured at Clapham Junction on 23 October 1967, was a regular performer on this route. *www.rail-online.co.uk*

ABOVE AND BELOW North British 'Warship' No D851 *Temeraire* is working 1M05, the 11.25 Penzance-Crewe van train, at Plymouth North Road on 16 August 1967. It went straight from the livery shown here into blue with full yellow ends in May 1968 after completion of an Intermediate overhaul that lasted two months. *Colin Moss*

ABOVE On the same day 'Warship' No D865 *Zealous* waits time with 'The Cornishman'. This was the last 'Warship' built by North British, entering traffic in June 1962. The maroon livery was applied in November 1965 and lasted until August 1969. 'The Cornishman' ran from Bradford Exchange to Penzance, diesel-hydraulic traction replacing a 'Peak' at Bristol Temple Meads. *Colin Moss*

TOP LEFT 'Western' No D1007 *Western Talisman* awaits departure from Plymouth on 16 August 1967, heading for Penzance with a train from Paddington. At this time most Paddington-Penzance services employed the same locomotive throughout. The 1S33 headcode must have caused some amusement and confusion to signalmen en route, with the train apparently destined for Scotland! This locomotive would come to grief on 19 December 1973 when a loose battery box cover came into contact with catch points at Ealing Broadway while working a Paddington-Oxford evening commuter service. *Colin Moss*

BOTTOM LEFT On the same day North British Type 2 No D6310 trundles through North Road on a St Blazey-Tavistock Junction Yard working. No D6310 had been a Laira locomotive from new but had been transferred to Newton Abbot in June 1967, together with D6311, to replace Nos D6320 and D6321, which moved from Newton Abbot to Bristol Bath Road. The wagons are LNER-built steel opens typically used in this period on engineering or demolition and recovery work, as they were relatively easy to load from the ground. *Colin Moss*

ABOVE 'Hymek' No D7079 was photographed at Plymouth, also on 16 August 1967, coupled to No D1017 *Western Warrior* in blue livery with small yellow warning panels, which it had received the previous February. The two locomotives had just arrived in the platform, presumably from Laira, and quickly headed back in the same direction. 'Hymek' appearances at Plymouth were infrequent, and they were even more rare in Cornwall, primarily because only a few Laira drivers were trained on them and none were allocated there after 1967. Although they would mainly be seen in the area on freight work, they did have a regular passenger diagram in the early 1970s on the Kensington Olympia to St Austell 'Motorail' service and were observed on summer Saturday trains. No D7032 had been trialled on the North Cornwall line to Wadebridge and Padstow. As for No D1017, it was destined to be one of the four consecutively numbered class members not to be air-braked and was withdrawn early. Note also the Royal Mail TPO coach on the left, resplendent in Post Office red. *Colin Moss*

LEFT Class 22 No D6333, seen at Aller Junction on 29 December 1967, is clearly not working train 1CO8, despite its headcode. It is heading along the main line towards the Paignton and Kingswear branch on one of the local DBV (Diesel and Brake Van) trips, probably destined for the gas works at Paignton. No D6333 was one of the last four Class 22s in traffic, together with Nos D6336, D6338 and D6339. Although officially withdrawn on 31 December 1971, the locomotive was noted working the 16.35 Torrington to Exeter milk train on 1 January 1972. On 3 January Class 25 No 5180 left St Blazey hauling Nos D6336 and D6338; calling at Exeter, it collected Nos D6333 and D6339 and all four were taken to St Phillip's Marsh. *www.rail-online.co.uk*

RIGHT No D6339 is at Heathfield on 29 December 1967 working 9D40, conveying china clay from Watts, Blakes & Bearne, one of the Newton Abbot trip freights covering the branches to Heathfield, Paignton and Kingswear. No D6339 was a Newton Abbot locomotive from November 1964 until May 1971, when it was sent to Laira. It was withdrawn on 3 October 1971 and actually went to Marsh Junction, coupled to No D6330. However, it was reprieved and returned to traffic on 17 October (although its official date of return was the 25th). In fact, it survived right to the end, working on 1 January 1972, on milk trips from Exeter together with No D6333. The last train to Heathfield was also hauled by a North British locomotive, 'Warship' No 857 on Sunday 3 October 1971, recovering track from the closed branch. *www.rail-online.co.uk*

1968

ABOVE No D6327, one of four of the class to wear blue livery with small yellow warning panels and seen at Old Oak Common probably in 1968, shows the four-section folding front communicating door that replaced the original two-part doors when the route indicator boxes were fitted. The modified locomotives had horizontal grab handles above the indicator boxes, whereas the later build had vertical handles. Other details visible are the cast 81A shed plate on the front skirting, the yellow route availability disc and the holder for the driver's name – the latter were removed on the later blue repaints to avoid interference with the double arrow emblem, which was positioned immediately below the cab window. In this early version of the blue livery there was a single small double arrow positioned high in the centre of the bodyside. *www.rail-online.co.uk*

LEFT No D7066 has been stripped to the bare bones at Swindon Works on 24 March 1968, with looms of wire hanging from the cab and engine compartment. It would emerge repainted in Rail Blue with full yellow ends. No D7066 was originally allocated to Cardiff Canton, moving to Old Oak Common in June 1965 and remaining there until withdrawal on 23 November 1971 with collision damage. *www.rail-online.co.uk*

ABOVE 'Teddy Bear' No D9521 basks in the summer sunshine at Margam in 1968. Luckily this one survives in private ownership following a period of industrial service at Ashington. The April 969 *Railway Observer* reported that on 14 February 1969 Nos D9521 and D9538 were both at Margam and summarised the remaining Class 14 diagrams in South Wales, opining that the class was unlikely to survive after March. There was one duty listed from Margam – the 03.40 to Glyncorrwg – which was transferred to a 350hp shunter working the following month (utilising a locomotive that had become spare when the Bridgend pilot duty was withdrawn in January), thus bringing to an end Margam-based Class 14 workings. No D9521 was in store at Landore by March 1969, withdrawn on 24 April and 'moved to Canton later in that year'. *www.rail-online.co.uk*

ABOVE No D7093 is at Cardiff Canton on 1 June 1968 in company with Nos D7083 and D7063, at a time when the depot was crowded with 'Hymeks'. Behind is Brush Type 4 No D1554, a visitor from Immingham. The difference in the application of the full yellow ends to the 'Hymeks' is shown on the right; No D7083 has the paint extended further round than on No D7063, which was the style used on the earlier 1967 and 1968 repaints. No D7063 found fame as the subject of the Triang, later Hornby, 'Hymek' model. *www.rail-online.co.uk*

ABOVE No D1025 heads a Class 4 fitted freight at Bradford Junction, near Bath, in June 1968. *Western Guardsman* was in this livery for just 12 months, from January 1968 until January 1969. *www.rail-online.co.uk*

LEFT No D814 *Dragon*, at Penzance in July 1968, had been repainted in blue with full yellow ends, double insignia, serif numbers and the 'D' prefix in August 1967. This arrangement lasted until its final livery change in May 1969, when it gained the later sans-serif numerals and lost its 'D' prefix. *Dragon* has the multiple working equipment that was refitted for double-headed workings in 1968. The locomotive was withdrawn at the end of 1971 but was one of three Class 42s reinstated in March 1972. It is displaying the 3A67 headcode, which was for the 16.55 St Erth-Kensington milk train, and it is likely that No D814 had worked this on the previous day as far as Plymouth, then worked back down to Penzance overnight. *www.rail-online.co.uk*

RIGHT 'Warship' No D866 *Zebra*, with No D823 *Hermes*, prepares to depart from Penzance in July 1968 with the 10.15 'Cornish Riviera Express' to Paddington. The mix of tatty green and maroon liveries is somewhat short of the BR Corporate image for the Western Region's prestige train! *Zebra* went into Swindon later in the month for an Intermediate overhaul, emerging in blue with full yellow ends. *Hermes*, maroon since May 1966, had only acquired the full yellow ends a couple of months earlier and did not go into blue until September 1969.

www.rail-online.co.uk

LEFT No D809 *Champion* passes Long Rock, Penzance, on a summer Saturday with 3A97, the 15.40 Penzance-Paddington perishables. This was the 19.20 ex-Plymouth on every other day of the week, and was booked for two Class 42s. The four-character train identification indicators had been fitted in February 1964, and No D809 was repainted in maroon with a small yellow warning panel in March 1966, the full yellow ends being applied two years later. *www.rail-online.co.uk*

RIGHT No D831 *Monarch* is seen at Long Rock depot in July 1968. We believe this to be the Hayle branch trip, with brake vans at each end and the Associated Octel chemical tank from the works at Hayle. The train is on the down main, possibly about to cross over or shunt back into the sidings. The traffic from Hayle was formed into the afternoon Ponsandane to Tavistock Junction freight service, picking up en route at Drump Lane, Truro and St Austell. On 30 November 1966 *Monarch* had been the second 'Warship' to emerge from Swindon in the new Rail Blue livery. Unlike the first, No D864 *Zambesi*, which had the prescribed full yellow ends, *Monarch* had for some reason reverted to small yellow warning panels. It eventually received the standard Corporate Blue in March 1969 and was withdrawn in October 1971. *www.rail-online.co.uk*

ABOVE Two locally resident 'Hymeks' on shed at Bristol Bath Road in the late autumn of 1968 are Nos D7006 and D7015; the latter has minor accident damage. Both were delivered without yellow warning panels, with No D7006 remaining in the livery shown here until withdrawn on 2 September 1971, the first of the class, together with No D7081, to be withdrawn. No D7015 moved to Old Oak Common in January 1972, but was withdrawn at Bath Road on 7 June that year following collision damage. *www.rail-online.co.uk*

LEFT Crewe-built No D1040
Western Queen stands at Laira
in July 1968. This was the
first of the class to receive
serious accident damage when
it was involved in a collision at
Knowle & Dorridge in August
1963 while deputising for a
Blue Pullman set. 'Her
Majesty' remained in maroon
with small warning panels
until 1970. *www.rail-online.co.uk*

RIGHT No D1030 *Western
Musketeer* passes Tiverton
Junction on 11 August
1968 with the 13.12 St
Erth-Kensington milk train.
Corporate Blue with a small
yellow panel was only worn by
seven of the class, including
Western Musketeer from
August 1966 to March
1970; after two years the
cab front is looking tatty. *www.
rail-online.co.uk*

LEFT No D7096 on a local freight passes through Cardiff General in the gloom of a December 1968 afternoon. The 'Hymek' had been transferred to Canton in April 1966, its second spell there – it had been there for three months from new in December 1963. No D7096 was repainted in blue for its final years in service, and following withdrawal in December 1972 it went, together with No D7076, after more than 18 months in storage at St Phillip's Marsh, to the Research Centre at Derby. It was not so fortunate as its now preserved classmate and was cut up in 1986 after the Centre had finished with it. *www.rail-online.co.uk*

ABOVE Blue-liveried No D7064 is caught near West Drayton on a fast fitted train including a continental van. In the background between the trees just right of centre and hidden by the train is the Nestlé factory, which sits just north of the Western Region main line. *www.rail-online.co.uk*

LEFT In around 1968 No D7048 stands at Swindon shed next to oil-stained Brush Type 4 No D1903. The 'Hymek' was badly damaged in a derailment at Spetchley, near Worcester, on 13 July 1969 when it fell part-way down an embankment. Surprisingly it was not withdrawn, and returned to service in blue with full yellow ends; it worked until the start of 1972, being officially withdrawn on 7 January at Reading. *www.rail-online.co.uk*

RIGHT One of the three 'Hymeks' painted blue including the area around the cab windows, No D7007 works the 11.15 Paddington to Worcester train through Pangbourne, just north of Reading, believed to be in 1968. *www.rail-online.co.uk*

1969

TOP LEFT 'Hymek' No D7034, seen here at Worcester on 7 April 1969, spent its early years at Cardiff Canton before it was transferred to Old Oak Common in August 1965. It was withdrawn from there in January 1972, one of no fewer than 25 'Hymeks' taken out of service that month, and remained there until July, when it went to Swindon for scrapping. It was the first of the class to be delivered with headboard clips, which can be seen at the top of the yellow warning panel. *www.rail-online.co.uk*

BOTTOM LEFT No D841 *Roebuck*, pictured on the same day at Worcester, had been transferred to Old Oak Common from Newton Abbot in October 1967. The depot's North British 'Warships' were used on Worcester line services from January 1968, taking over fully from May when the new timetable came into operation. In early 1968 an attempt was made by Old Oak Common to try and improve the poor cab ventilation on the D833s allocated there by cutting two circular ventilation holes below the route indicator panels. *Roebuck* is in the first version of blue with full yellow ends received in September 1967, and has the double arrow insignia on both cabs, old-style serif numerals, a black background to its nameplates, and retains the 'D' prefix. No D841 has a TOPS panel, but its shed plate is still on the side skirting. *www.rail-online.co.uk*

BELOW No D9515 was completed at Swindon Works in October 1964, but its stay on the Western Region was short; it was transferred to Hull Dairycoates in January 1967, arriving on 18 January together with Nos D9541, D9548 and D9549 travelling behind Class 47 No D1572. It was sold from Hull to the British Steel Corporation-owned Buckminster Ironstone Quarries at High Dyke in November 1968 and lasted there until 1972, when the quarries closed; it was then transferred to BSC Corby for similar duties. When that complex closed in 1980 No D9515 was sold to Spain for further use, being re-gauged at Hunslet of Leeds and exported via Goole Docks in June 1982. However, it is believed that it was never used in Spain and was noted out of use at Madrid Chamartin in 1984. *www.rail-online.co.uk*

LEFT This was a typical mid-week scene in the late 1960s at Exeter Stabling Point, in this view looking from the buffer stops. A DMU is in for refuelling and a maroon 'Western' with full yellow ends is idling away in the distance. No D6333 was the last of the first production batch of D6300s to be built without headcode boxes, and was only modified in 1967 when it was repainted in blue with full yellow ends. It would spend its last couple of years pottering around the local branches, perhaps collecting a few milk tanks from the dairies, and was one of the last four Class 22s to be withdrawn on 1 January 1972.
www.rail-online.co.uk

RIGHT No D7009, seen at Westbury on 8 June 1969, sports a livery that definitely did not suit the 'Hymeks', particularly when the yellow front was extended around the sides of the cab. It was one of those 'Hymeks' that failed regularly in traffic in its final days, withdrawal coming in May 1973; after storage at Bristol St Phillip's Marsh and Laira, No D7009 finally made it to Swindon Works on 18 December 1973, and had been broken up by the following October.
www.rail-online.co.uk

LEFT No D7075 is at Landore in around 1969 with what looks like a trip working of fuel oil. This 'Hymek' was based in South Wales from August 1966 until October 1971, when it was transferred to Bristol Bath Road. It was withdrawn on 6 May 1973 after a transmission failure the previous month and was scrapped at Birds, Long Marston, in early 1974. *www.rail-online.co.uk*

ABOVE When Class 35 No D7052 was photographed at Margam depot on 1 June 1969, it was allocated to Cardiff Canton, but moved to Old Oak Common in May 1971, where it worked until the end of the year before being placed into store. It was reinstated by Canton twice in the following year, from March to July and again on 21 October, before finally being taken out of service on 12 November. *www.rail-online.co.uk*

RIGHT A nice view of No D6323 from the concrete footbridge at Laira in 1969. The staining on the central bodyside was caused by an anti-corrosion inhibitor that was added to the boiler water feed and engine cooling water, and which escaped in the steam that emerged when the steam generator safety valve lifted, leaving the condensed water to run down the side of the locomotive. It was extremely effective at removing paint and also the skin of shed staff who came into contact with it. *www.rail-online.co.uk*

ABOVE No D6323, seen at Laira in 1969, had spent its short life in the West Country, returning to its first depot at Plymouth in September 1968 after spells at Newton Abbot and Bristol Bath Road. It was stored in April 1971 prior to withdrawal on 22 May. It has a blue TOPS panel below the NBL maker's plate and a blue 84A depot sticker to the right of the cab door. *www.rail-online.co.uk*

LEFT On 22 February 1967 the Chief Engineer (Traction & Rolling Stock) stated that 'there is considerable pressure ... for the earliest and widest adoption of the enlarged yellow treatment, and in view of the important safety aspect I should be obliged if you would arrange to apply this to locomotives being repainted or extensively touched up, in advance of the adoption of the new livery, and receipt of the latest painting diagrams.' All subsequent blue repaints had full yellow ends and these were also applied to two green-liveried locomotives, No D808 *Centaur* and No D810 *Cockade*, in late 1967. The latter is pictured at Dawlish on an up local in 1969-70.

RIGHT No D6328 is engaged on track recovery work at Witney on Sunday 14 December 1969. The remainder of the Fairford branch as far as Witney had closed on 2 November, with the last passenger train, a nine-car railtour worked by a DMU, the 'Witney Wanderer', running two days earlier. Class 22s had been used on the Witney branch since January 1966, working the thrice-weekly freight, and at least 13 members of the class are known to have worked to Witney. No D6326 was used to take away the last remaining stock from the branch before the gangs moved in to remove the rails. No D6328 was stopped on 28 June 1971 for examination at Laira, and on 8 July was released and put into store serviceable, but was withdrawn on the 17th. *www.rail-online.co.uk*

4 The early 1970s

1970

ABOVE Maroon-liveried North British-built 'Warship' No D844 *Spartan* stands at Old Oak Common in March 1970 alongside 'Hymek' No D7026 still in its original two-tone green. The significant improvement in the front-end appearance as a result of the Design Panel's input to the later design is apparent. No D844 would be repainted in blue when it went into Swindon for an Intermediate repair in October, and has the Old Oak modification of the two circular ventilation holes below the route indicator panels, a blanked-off air intake, a blue-backed TOPS panel and a stencilled 81A depot code to the right of the cab door. *www.rail-online.co.uk*

TOP RIGHT No D7009 eases slowly past the engineering work at Dr Day's Bridge Junction, Bristol, on Thursday 2 April 1970. This was part of the Bristol area multiple-aspect signalling

installation that took place between October 1969 and February 1971. The photograph was taken from Barrow Road bridge with Temple Meads station in the right distance. The junction was named after Dr William Edward Day, who lived in Barrow Road. The working timetable used the name 'Dr Day's Junction', whereas the signal box is named 'Dr Day's Bridge Junction Signal Box'. There was a triangular junction with the Bristol avoiding line, known as the 'Rhubarb' loop, after the pub on the left-hand side next to the railway; this line is just visible in the bottom left of the picture, diverging from the main Bristol to Bath main line that runs from left to right, while the 'Hymek' is on the South Wales line. There were 21 carriage sidings in the distance, spread over both sides of the tracks towards Temple Meads. The Class 35's train includes a large number of brake vans, which suggests it may be a return trip working. A Class 22 heads the engineering train on the left, and the relaid track looks almost ready for use. *www.rail-online.co.uk*

RIGHT Two Class 14s, No D9519 with No D9509 behind, are seen at Cardiff Canton on 10 May 1970. Withdrawn in September 1968, the former was stored under tarpaulins at Canton from then until March 1970, only to be refurbished in order to work at Hereford in April and May 1970. After this it was returned to Canton for more storage and would go for scrap that December to Cohen's at Kettering.
www.rail-online.co.uk

LEFT No D9509 was also photographed at Canton on the same day. It had been withdrawn in October 1968 after only four years in service, some of which was spent in store due to insufficient work. Like No D9519 it was stored at Canton under tarpaulins from then until March 1970, only then going inside for further storage. It too went to Cohen's for scrap in December.
www.rail-online.co.uk

LEFT No D1025 *Western Guardsman* was also at Canton on 10 May 1970, together with Brush Type 4 No 1599 and no fewer than seven 'Hymeks', including No D7060 in green, No D7056 in blue with a small yellow warning panel, and No D7066 in the final livery with full yellow ends.
www.rail-online.co.uk

ABOVE No D6320, present at Canton on the same day, was the 'celebrity' North British Type 2. In 1968 Gloucester Horton Road shed had bestowed on it the name Lister, using a red box label with white letters which came from the Lister factory at Dursley that made industrial engines. The label, which was on only one side of the locomotive, was positioned below the BR emblem and lasted until the end of 1969, local spotters having picked away pieces until there was little of it left! The Types 2s were never common at Canton; the locomotives just worked in from Gloucester or Bristol and none was ever allocated to Welsh sheds.
www.rail-online.co.uk

ABOVE The compact lines of the 'Hymeks' are well illustrated by blue-liveried No D7056 at Bedminster near Bristol with a local freight working on 27 May 1970. It worked until January 1972, and after a period at St Phillip's Marsh was cut up at Swindon by the middle of the year. *www.rail-online.co.uk*

RIGHT 'Warships' Nos D861 *Vigilant* and 868 *Zephyr* have arrived at the end of the line at Penzance on 21 June 1970 with the 07.10 Exeter to Penzance train. Since 4,400hp is somewhat excessive for a six-vehicle stopping passenger train, it was probably a positioning working to bring one of the two locomotives from Laira using a single crew and taking up a single timetable path. No 868 never carried maroon livery and was in its first style of blue with full yellow ends; it had two double arrow insignia, serif numbers and no 'D' prefix, whereas No D861 is still in maroon with a small yellow warning panel, which it had from September 1966 until repainted blue in March 1971. Both locomotives were withdrawn in the great cull of hydraulics in October 1971, when 29 'Warships' were taken out of service. *www.rail-online.co.uk*

ABOVE No D1039 *Western King*, seen at Laira in 1970, carried this livery from April 1968 to February 1971. It was one of the locomotives fitted with experimental rotary windscreen wipers, but these had been removed in October 1964. It was to receive another experiment, a modified rectangular air grille, which it kept until withdrawn. *Western King* was the second Class 52 to be stopped when it was taken out of traffic on 28 February 1973, but was not withdrawn until July. It stood decaying on the dump at Laira until December after both bogies had been used on No D1038; both engines were also re-used. Together with No D1042, it was the first of the dual air-braked and dual AWS-fitted locomotives to be withdrawn, the four members of the class not so equipped having preceded them in May and June. *www.rail-online.co.uk*

ABOVE In order to save paths, locomotives travelling between depots for other work were often booked to pilot passenger trains. One such train was 1E30, the 08.00 Plymouth-Leeds, on which the pilot locomotive was booked to be 'attached' from Plymouth to Bristol, where it would later continue light to Severn Tunnel Junction to work freights from South Wales to the capital at Acton and Hither Green. Hence this photograph of a 'Warship' working a train with a diesel-electric, as No 810 *Cockade* stands in Platform 7 at Bristol Temple Meads after arrival from Plymouth. The driver is about to climb on board the 'Warship' to go onto Bath Road depot, as the Class 45's driver scrambles up to take the train northwards to Leeds. *www.rail-online.co.uk*

1971

TOP LEFT No D809 *Champion* received maroon livery with full yellow ends in March 1968 and was a regular on the Exeter-Waterloo service. On 1 July 1971 it is ready to depart from Central with the 12.30 train to Waterloo, having been used earlier in the day to work trip freights from Riverside Yard to the yard at Central, shunting the wagons in the background.

www.rail-online.co.uk

LEFT Type 2 No 6326, heading 6B73, the 14.23 Exeter to Tiverton and Hemyock milk train at Tiverton Junction on Saturday 10 July 1971, is passed by maroon work-stained 'Warship' No D809 *Champion*, working 1M49, the 14.15 Newton Abbot-Sutton Coldfield 'Motorail' service. The Type 2 is in the final version of blue applied to the Class 22s, with Rail Alphabet sans-serif numerals below the double arrows, and would be withdrawn within three months, on the same day as No D809. *www.rail-online.co.uk*

ABOVE No D6337 arrives at Newton Abbot on 2 July 1971, having worked 6B05, the 20.00 Waterston to Heathfield Gulf fuel tanks, which were of 45-ton capacity and air-braked only, hence the brake van. Having deposited the tanks at the Distribution Depot at Heathfield, No D6337 is returning the brake van to Newton Abbot. As one of the second production batch, it had the flush type of route indicator boxes from new, and two-piece corridor doors. It has the early version of the Corporate Blue livery with the old-pattern serif numbers still with the 'D' prefix, which indicates that it had been repainted in 1967. It was always based in the West Country, initially at Newton Abbot, then Bristol Bath Road from July 1966 until September 1967, when it returned to 83A. Its final posting was Laira in January 1970, and it was withdrawn three months after this picture was taken, going initially to St Phillip's Marsh before being moved to Swindon for cutting up in March 1972. *www.rail-online.co.uk*

RIGHT Type 2 No 6348, pictured at the Laira 'Dump' on 25 July 1971, had been withdrawn the previous day. It had been stopped on the 13th, needing a new transmission, but this was not authorised and the locomotive was stored. '7A08' refers to its working on 2 July, assisting No D827 from Plymouth to Exeter on the St Blazey to Acton freight. No 6348 remained at Laira until October, when it was moved to St Phillip's Marsh before going to Swindon for cutting up in March 1972. It was one of 12 of the second production series to receive blue livery and one of four to have the final variant with Rail Alphabet sans-serif numerals, no 'D' prefix and double arrows above the numbers. No D1011 *Western Thunderer*, on the next road, would work for another four years, until October 1975.

www.rail-online.co.uk

LEFT This sad line-up of four D6300s and 'Warship' No D864 *Zambesi* is at Swindon on 14 August 1971. No D6312, on the extreme left, was one of only two Class 22s to have full yellow ends while in green livery, the other being No D6331. It had been withdrawn in October 1968, whereas No 6352, in the centre of the photograph, had stayed in traffic until May 1971. The latter is in the final version of Corporate Blue with double arrows on both cabs positioned above sans-serif numerals without the 'D' prefix. To the right are Nos D6309 and D6307, both withdrawn earlier in the year in green livery with small yellow warning panels. *www.rail-online.co.uk*

ABOVE Class 42 No 824 *Highflyer*, parked in the sidings at Waterloo, is ready to work the 19.08 Waterloo-Exeter train, probably on Saturday 4 September 1971, having brought up the Saturdays-only 11.05 train from Exeter. The white diamonds, signifying the retention of multiple working fittings, are clearly visible. The picture was taken from an unusual angle, with the Post Office tower in the left background and a very decrepit ex-Southern Railway 'Parcels and Miscellaneous Van' (probably in internal user service) behind the 'Warship'. *www.rail-online.co.uk*

LEFT Class 35 No D7051, seen at Tiverton Junction on Saturday 28 August 1971, is heading 6B33, the 03.50 Acton to Exeter Riverside Yard mixed goods train, including new Howard agricultural equipment on Lowfits. Together with Nos D7007 and D7004, this locomotive had received this rather unattractive version of the early blue livery at the end of November 1966. From the middle of the following month, Swindon started to add the white window frames to the 'Hymek' repaints, No D7010 becoming the first recipient. *www.rail-online.co.uk*

RIGHT Another picture of No D7051 in 1971 shows it arriving at London Paddington. It was one of the three 'Hymeks' painted in blue without the beneficial effect of white around the cab windows, and retained this livery until withdrawal on 1 January 1972. It had not worked since failing with transmission faults on 2 December 1971 at Worcester, working 1C06, the 18.15 Paddington to Hereford train. Hauled to Bristol on the 6th, it was side-lined awaiting repairs that never materialised. *www.rail-online.co.uk*

LEFT In the blue livery applied at the start of 1971, North British 'Warship' No 844 *Spartan* arrives at Paddington in the summer of that year with the 07.10 Hereford-Paddington train. Commonly associated with the Class 43 'Warships', this particular train over the Cotswolds was booked to be worked by a Bath Road-based Class 47 at this time. Although withdrawn on 4 October 1971, when all the remaining Class 43s were taken out of service, *Spartan* travelled from store at Bristol St Phillip's Marsh to Worcester later that month for carriage-heating duties before finally running under its own power to Swindon for scrapping on 26 November. *www.rail-online.co.uk*

RIGHT Two D6300s withdrawn in green with small yellow panels, No D6307 nearest the camera and No D6309 beyond, await their fate next to Class 43 'Warship' No D864 *Zambesi* at Swindon on 11 August 1971. The latter had been the first 'Warship' to be painted in British Railways Rail Blue, with a brown underframe and bogies, in November 1966. Amazingly, the diamond-shaped NBL maker's plates are still on the two Type 2s.

www.rail-online.co.uk

LEFT Two withdrawn Class 43s at Swindon on 14 August 1971 show the subtle variations in the Corporate Blue livery. No D864 *Zambesi* on the left has an earlier version with serif-style numbers dating back to May 1967. No D860 *Victorious*, which was repainted in February 1968, has Rail Alphabet sans-serif numbers and a slightly thicker and shorter double arrow emblem. Both had been withdrawn in March 1971 and were brought to Swindon for cutting in June of that year. *www.rail-online.co.uk*

RIGHT With two exceptions, all of the 'Warship' repaints were done at Swindon; in mid-1971 the paintwork of two locomotives was in such an appalling state that they were repainted at Laira. When No 826 *Jupiter* was stopped for engine and transmission changes in June its paintwork was so bad that the original lining band from its days in green was showing through. The double arrow symbols were hand-painted and the serif numbers, without the 'D' prefix, were not level, as can be seen in this picture taken after its withdrawal at St Phillip's Marsh on 30 October 1971. *www.rail-online.co.uk*

1972

RIGHT St Philip's Marsh had a long history of being used to store withdrawn steam locos, and this would continue through the hydraulic era starting with the 'Warships' and the North British Type 2s. No 6319, seen here in a line with Nos D6328 and 6348, both withdrawn in July 1971, was the last of the class to be overhauled at Swindon, emerging on 12 June 1971 and withdrawn at Laira just 12 weeks later in September. On its left, No D6328 shows the earlier style of blue livery with an old-type serif 'D'-prefixed number positioned above the double arrow, whereas Nos 6319 and 6348 have the final sans-serif style without the 'D' prefix, the symbol above the number, and the TOPS panel below. No 6319 should have been preserved, but was cut up after a mix-up between Swindon and Derby, the latter failing to communicate the fact that it had accepted a bid from the late Colin Massingham for the Type 2, which was barely run in after its General overhaul. *www.rail-online.co.uk*

BELOW No 806 *Cambrian* passes through Andover with a train of stone empties from Gatwick to Westbury. The Gatwick stone trains ran round at Woking and often ran with incorrect headcodes as a result. The headcode '6014' would have applied for the outward journey, the 08.55 from Westbury to Gatwick, making this 6V83, the 16.49 return. Three other members of the class, Nos 814, 825 and 829, which had previously been withdrawn on New Year's Day 1972, were reinstated in March 1972 because of the increase in this stone traffic. *Cambrian* only received blue livery in March 1971 after wearing maroon for almost five years. *www.rail-online.co.uk*

LEFT No 814, formerly *Dragon*, runs through Exeter St David's with a short train of milk tanks forming the 17.15 from Lapford on 20 June 1972. It had been withdrawn on 1 January that year, and the nameplates would have been quickly removed, but was reinstated to traffic on 25 March, before being finally withdrawn in November. No 814 is in its final livery acquired in May 1969, with white diamonds on the buffer beam denoting the multiple working equipment that was refitted for the double-headed workings in 1968. *www.rail-online.co.uk*

RIGHT No 824 *Highflyer* waits in the through line at Exeter St David's on 21 June 1972 with 6B16, the 17.15 Lapford-Exeter milk tanks. The locomotive is showing the '6A27' headcode from its previous day's duty, the 11.55 Malago-Old Oak van train. No 824 went from green into this final version of blue, emerging in this livery from a Classified repair in April 1969. It was one of the last three to be withdrawn, in December 1972. *www.rail-online.co.uk*

5 The final years, 1973-77

1973

ABOVE No D1040 *Western Queen* is on milk train duties at Par, some time in the early 1970s. 6A21 was the 16.40 St Erth-Acton milk train and was often loaded heavily. If an additional service was required, 6A19, the 13.50 St Erth-Acton, would run, mostly during spring and autumn when the Cornish grass was growing strongly! *www.rail-online.co.uk*

RIGHT The passenger leaning out of the window as No 1025 *Western Guardsman* departs from Birmingham New Street in 1974 is unlikely to be a 1st Class gricer! There is no 'D' on the number plate, and note that No 1025 has the Laira allocation sticker next to the door much higher than usual. As seen here *Guardsman* also ran with several knocks and scratches in its final year and was one of the few 'Westerns' to be withdrawn

by simply switching it off at the end of the 1975 summer timetable. The Rotunda tower in the background is disfigured by the large Double Diamond sign. *www.rail-online.co.uk*

1974

RIGHT No 7093 is seen at Swindon on 2 February 1974 heading 6A27, the 11.55 goods from Malago Vale, Bristol, to Old Oak Common. Its washed-out blue paintwork came from passing too many times through the carriage wash at Old Oak! The 'Siphon G' parcels van was designed by the GWR for milk traffic, but has been transferred to Enparts service moving stores between the various locomotive depots from Swindon Works, although it is still in Corporate Blue from its parcels days. *www.rail-online.co.uk*

BELOW Very soon to be withdrawn, on the 19th of the following month, and fresh from its Swindon Works Open Day display, No 7093 is seen again at Didcot in September 1974 on an Engineers' trip working. The last remaining 'Hymeks' spent much of their time on parcels or departmental duties, but not usually in the company of a diesel-electric, which would require two crews. The silver buffers originate from the Open Day on

7 September, when No 7093 stood in for steam locomotive No 6000 *King George V* on a Pullman car shuttle service that operated within the Works complex. *www.rail-online.co.uk*

LEFT Type 1 No D9536 was completed in March 1965 and withdrawn from Severn Tunnel Junction in April 1969. The virtually just 'run-in' locomotive was stored at Landore goods yard and Cardiff Canton before sale to the NCB in March 1970 for use on the Ashington Colliery system. Here it is seen on 19 June 1974 passing its home shed at Ashington. It received a Heavy overhaul at the NCB Lambton Engine Works, but was out of use by March 1984, having put in 14 years of industrial service compared to its four with BR. *www.rail-online.co.uk*

RIGHT No D9523 was completed in November 1964 and after working at Old Oak Common and Bristol Bath Road was one of those selected for transfer to the North Eastern Region at Hull Dairycoates in January 1967 for use on the trip freights from the yards to the docks complex. As traffic quickly declined, No D9523 was stored inside Dairycoates roundhouse. Withdrawal came in April 1968 and it was then sold to Stewarts & Lloyds for use at the company's Glendon East Ironstone Quarries, arriving there in December. It is seen there in the early 1970s, with the Midland line to Melton in the distance, before renumbering, which occurred around 1974. When the quarries closed it moved to BSC Gretton Brook in May 1980, but was at the BSC disposal site in the steelworks by December. No D9523 was sold for preservation in October 1981 and has since worked at Loughborough and at the **Nene Valley Railway.** *www.rail-online.co.uk*

ABOVE No 1021 *Western Cavalier* approaches Reading in 1974 with the 13.30 Paddington to Penzance service. It has a fresh coat of paint on the cab front as part of its October 1974 Laira depot repaint; this included painting out the 'D' prefix. *www.rail-online.co.uk*

RIGHT No D1015 *Western Champion* leaves Bristol Temple Meads in 1974 with postal and newspaper empties from Temple Meads Goods to Old Oak Common, via Swindon, consisting of a number of ex-GWR 'Siphon Gs'. The signal box is still in BR(W) 'chocolate and cream'. *Western Champion* would almost make it to the final end of the class, not being withdrawn until 12 December 1976 after a derailment at Castle Cary while working a Westbury to Yeovil freight. Train 4A71 was also used to move defective locomotive components from Bristol Bath Road to Swindon Works for repair using the 'Siphon Gs' marked 'ENPARTS'. *www.rail-online.co.uk*

1975

RIGHT No D9507 was withdrawn from Hull Dairycoates at the end of March 1968 and stayed there until November, when it was sold to Stewarts & Lloyds of Corby, becoming that company's No 35. It was renumbered 55 in October 1974 and is seen at Gretton Brook shed, which housed the locomotives working on the iron ore mineral trains. It worked at Corby until the end of 1980, when the steelworks closed. *www.rail-online.co.uk*

ABOVE No D9530, seen at Canton in October 1975, was probably there for tyre turning while en route to NCB Maerdy Colliery from its former owner at Gulf Oil Waterston. Gulf Oil had purchased it from Canton in September 1969, and it served at Maerdy until cut up for scrap in the spring of 1982. *www.rail-online.co.uk*

LEFT No D1068 *Western Reliance* emerges from the gloom of Platform 1 at Birmingham New Street in 1975 past a group of spotters wearing pumps and flares. Train reporting number 1V28 was the 10.25 New Street-Paddington service, which was the return working of the 06.45 from Paddington to Birmingham. The locomotive would probably have worked one of the overnight services from the West Country into Paddington before heading for the Midlands. *www.rail-online.co.uk*

RIGHT No D1026 *Western Centurion* is waiting in the centre road at Exeter St David's with a train of concrete-sleepered track, probably from the Pre-Assembly Depot at Taunton, as No D1015 *Western Champion* departs with 1B45, the 11.30 Paddington to Penzance 'Cornish Riviera Express'. No D1026's train would be heading for Hackney Yard at Newton Abbot, where its load would be marshalled into trains for the next weekend's engineering jobs.
www.rail-online.co.uk

RIGHT No D1057 *Western Chieftain* passes the former LSWR station at Crediton in 1975 with a train from Meldon Quarry. The locomotive would remain in service until the following April.

www.rail-online.co.uk

LEFT No D1056 *Western Sultan* follows a Class 50 to Paddington with plenty of 'clag' as it leaves Reading in the summer of 1976. *Sultan* was one of those fitted with additional cab ventilation grilles and was unusual in helping out on the official farewell railtours in the final three months of the class. These were usually the preserve of Nos D1013 and D1023, but *Western Sultan* worked the 'Western China Clay' tour on 4 December 1976, only to be withdrawn 11 days later.

www.rail-online.co.uk

1976

RIGHT No D1048 *Western Lady* is at the head of a milk train in Exeter yard, down side, during the long hot summer of 1976. *Lady* could be identified by the large scrape at the bottom of the bodyside dating from a minor accident in 1972. It would never be repaired while in service, only when preserved! *www.rail-online.co.uk*

ABOVE On 21 February 1976 No D1068 *Western Reliance* passes the ruins of the Hallenbeagle copper mine, near the site of Scorrier station, a classic Cornish setting. There was no need to set headcodes from Sunday 4 January 1976, but perhaps the driver wanted everyone to know that he was working the 'Cornish Riviera Express'. *www.rail-online.co.uk*

ABOVE No D1068 *Western Reliance* is reflected in the water at Cockwood Harbour near Starcross as it heads for Exeter on a glorious Saturday 25 June 1976. The train is 1M01, the St Austell to Kensington Olympia 'Motorail' service. Having worked the outward equivalent from Kensington earlier that day, No D1068 started to run low on fuel on 1M01 and had to be topped by Class 50 No 50049 later in the journey. *www.rail-online.co.uk*

ABOVE No D1072 was fitted with experimental vertical windscreen wipers, but upon removal, unlike No D1056, only the horizontal 'runner' was retained. *Western Glory* is seen here at Truro on 17 July 1976 heading for Plymouth with 1A79, the 09.10 service from Falmouth to Paddington. No D1072 was one of the handful simply switched off at the end of the Summer 1976 timetable on 2 November, a planned withdrawal. *www.rail-online.co.uk*

1977

ABOVE No D1041 *Western Prince* comes to the end of the line at Penzance, and almost to the end of the hydraulic era, on 5 February 1977. By the 26th of that month the final 'Western' had been switched off for good, No D1041 itself succumbing a few days earlier after one engine failed at Liskeard. *www.rail-online.co.uk*